Miraculous Ideas

Thoughts on
A Course in Miracles

by Edwin Navarro

Miraculous Ideas

Thoughts on
A Course in Miracles

by Edwin Navarro

Published by Navarro Publishing

Copyright (c) 2014 Edwin Navarro

All Rights Reserved. No part of this book may be reproduced in any form without permission of the publisher, except by a reviewer who may quote brief passages in a review.

Excerpts from *A Course in Miracles* copyright (c) 1975, 1992, 1999 by Foundation for *A Course in Miracles*.

Cover design by thecovercounts.com

edwinnavarro.com

Also by Edwin Navarro,

It's All Mind: The Simplified Philosophy of A Course in Miracles

The End of Guilt: Realizing Your Innocence through A Course in Miracles

Roland's Quest: A Modern-Day Spiritual Journey

For the Seekers

Contents

Preface	1
Introduction - A Unique Course	3
Section I: The Fundamentals	
The Practice of Forgiveness	11
Looking for Love	17
Finding the Holy Spirit	22
There Is Only One Mind – And Only One Ego	29
Original Fear and Original Guilt	33
Section II: Thinking Differently	
Getting What You Deserve	41
A Course in Miracles and the Borg	46
It Used to Be Nice to Feel Special	51
"He's a God-Fearin' Man"	55
On the Death of Children	59
Section III: The Practical	
Can We Really Be Guiltless?	65
Nothing Is Unforgivable	70
The Ego and the Monkey Mind	74
But I Don't Want to Forgive!	80
Loving Everyone	85
Suggested Reading	90

Note: This book contains quotes from *A Course in Miracles*, which are referenced using the following shorthand,

First Letter – T for Text, W for Workbook, M for Manual

For Text quotes, the T is followed by the Chapter, Section, and Paragraph numbers.

For Workbook quotes, the W is followed by the Lesson and Paragraph numbers.

For Manual quotes, the M is followed by the Chapter and Paragraph numbers.

Examples: T-11.VI.7, W-169.5, M-21.1

Preface

Miraculous Ideas is a series of essays about *A Course in Miracles*. Some of these have appeared previously on my blog, 'The Philosophy of *A Course in Miracles*' at blog.edwinnavarro.com. Most of the essays have been expanded for this book and a number of new essays have been added.

The essays are roughly grouped into three sections, though the order is somewhat arbitrary except for the first one, 'The Practice of Forgiveness'. The reader may want to read this one before the others, since there are some important basic concepts about forgiveness covered here, and several of the other essays refer to this one. It contains a clear step-by-step process for applying forgiveness in your life, and once this process is mastered, it shows you how forgiveness can become a part of your everyday experience.

It is assumed the reader has some familiarity with the concepts of *A Course in Miracles*. If you do not understand some of the ideas or terms used in this book, it might be helpful to first read one or more of the books in the Suggested Reading section at the end of the book. The more you understand about the Course, the more you will get from these essays.

Above all, I hope the reader will find enjoyment here, maybe stretching your mind a bit and allowing you to see the world differently. I invite you to join me along this journey as we explore a few corners of the vastness that is *A Course in Miracles*. Plow on in and perhaps you will come away with a new appreciation of your own wonderful, powerful Mind.

Introduction - A Unique Course

> This is a manual for a special curriculum, ... a special form of the universal course. There are many thousands of other forms, all with the same outcome. They merely save time. (M-1.4)

A Course in Miracles is one of these thousands of forms. It does not say what the others are, but anyone who has experienced or studied other spiritual and religious traditions will quickly realize the Course is a unique form. It is unique in how it was created, its use of language, but most importantly in what it says. Its message is one of Hope and Love and Peace, but also a nonjudgmental look at where we've gone wrong. Its purpose is to teach us the way Home, back to our true place in God.

God

The God of the Course is Pure Oneness. This God can never be fully described using our dualistic language, but we have to do the best we can to convey the idea of God using this language. In this philosophy, we can look at four aspects of God as the foundation for what follows.

1 – God is All That Is, Everything. There is nothing that is not God.

2 – God is Mind, Thoughts, Ideas, and nothing but Mind.

3 – God is Pure Love. All thoughts of God are Loving.

4 – God is Creative. God is not static, but is in a constant state of Creation.

From this, there are several immediate conclusions. If God is Everything, then we are God. If God is Mind, then we are only

Miraculous Ideas

Mind. If God is Love, we are only Love. If God is Creative, then we are Creators.

In addition, if God is Everything, then believing there is something separate from God is an illusion. If God is Mind, then believing we live in an objective world separate from our mind is an illusion. If God is Pure Love, then God cannot be judgmental and punishing or remote and distant. If God is Creative, God, and our existence in God, is not boring or fixed or rigid.

In fact, our existence in God is one of Joy and Love and Peace and Creation. This is our True Home, and the world we believe we live in every day is an illusion. How did we get to this state, where we see fear and guilt and pain? How could we believe in this world when Joy and Love are our Natural State? It all comes down to the idea of separation.

The Idea of Separation

It begins with our Natural Existence in the Mind of God. Within this Mind, in some small corner, this idea could occur – What if we could be separate from God? The idea is absurd, since God is Everything, but it could be explored. This was the beginning of the world we experience today.

In order for some part of the Mind of God to believe it separated from God, it would have to imagine a 'God' very different from the True God, perhaps one that is judgmental, vengeful, or simply too distant to experience. This small part of the mind we will call the separated self, which is really just a collection of ideas all centered on maintaining the sense of separation.

In order for this separated self to distance itself from this 'God', it invents the idea of fear and begins to live in fear of retribution. It also invents the idea of guilt so it will further hide itself from the Love that is so near. Of course, some part of this separated self knows where it came from, it knows it is a Child of God, but the separated self tries to ignore that part. It then lives with a

Introduction - A Unique Course

split mind, one part connected to God and the other part focused on the separation. In the Course, the part that remembers where it came from is called the Holy Spirit. The other part, the part that works constantly to maintain the separation, is referred to as the ego.

The Ego

The ego has only one purpose and it will do everything it can to maintain the illusion of separation. Though the ego is part of the one separated self, it has created the illusion of billions of individuals, all separate and guilty and in fear. It has projected this fear and guilt out onto an illusory world we believe we live in. And it has created the illusion of the body we believe we are trapped in, a body that we must try to keep alive at all costs, even though that body's end is assured.

When we listen to the ego, we see those outside of us as a threat. We see this world we live in as threatening, and we build up our defenses emotionally, psychologically, and physically to prevent us from being harmed. Even within what seem to be our loving relationships, we experience anger, pain, and guilt because we still see the ones we believe we love as separate.

Through judgment, the ego teaches us how everyone is different and how those differences are a threat to us. The ego shows us how others' actions are often attacks. It shows us how our own actions sometimes result in others feeling pain, leading us to feelings of guilt. As long as we listen to the ego and only see the world the ego presents to us, we will feel trapped in a life that appears to lead ultimately to death.

Forgiveness

Fortunately, the Course also presents us with a way out of this illusion, a way beyond death and pain and fear. That way is through forgiveness, a forgiveness unlike what we may have learned through religion or psychology. This way leads to free-

Miraculous Ideas

dom from the ego's influence and reuniting with the Mind of God. This way leads us Home.

The common version of forgiveness starts with someone committing a perceived wrong on us. We feel we have been attacked in some way, whether that is physical or emotional or psychological. The purveyors of this brand of forgiveness suggest we should speak to this person and tell them how we feel about the actions that occurred, and then to release our feelings about this person so we don't feel trapped by our anger or hatred toward them.

The Course offers a very different brand of forgiveness. In the Course, God is All Mind and Pure Love, and that is our Natural State. Any attack we perceive must be an illusion, one projected by the ego to further its cause of separation. If we realize this attack is an illusion, we can be free of the feelings we have about the attack and therefore free of the illusion. This is what is meant by forgiveness in the Course – freeing ourselves from illusions.

Within our mind, the Holy Spirit, the part of the separated self that remembers its connection to God, is available to us. To the Holy Spirit, attacks, whether on us or by us, are impossible. Only one who believes in a body living in a physical world can perceive attacks on the body coming from the physical world. The Holy Spirit knows the body and this world do not exist, and therefore when we get in touch with this inner part of ourselves, we find the strength to free the illusion, to forgive.

The Goal of the Course

Through the practice of forgiveness, the Course offers us not only the possibility, but the inevitability of reaching a state of peace. Once we learn the way of forgiveness and put it into practice regularly, our mental state and even the world we inhabit will begin to change. When we reach a point where our first reaction in ev-

Introduction - A Unique Course

ery situation is to forgive, we will be in a state of continual forgiveness.

What this offers us is a state where we live our lives in touch with the Holy Spirit, where we learn to follow the way of the Holy Spirit in all our dealings in life, and where through a change in perception, the world we inhabit becomes a place of peace. Once we achieve that peace, it is ours and no one can take it away from us.

There will be a final step where we will slip away from this world, and all the illusions we have experienced here will fade away. We will find our way back Home, back to our Natural State of Being, back to our place within the Loving Mind of God.

Section I: The Fundamentals

The Practice of Forgiveness

"Practice?!" To most of us, the word practice elicits thoughts of drudgery and repetition, images from childhood of sitting for hours practicing scales on the piano, or standing at the foul line shooting hundreds of free throws, or yet one more plié at the ballet barre. We are taught that through practice we'll get better at something, and once we're good at it, it will ultimately be fun and rewarding.

For instance, in learning to play piano, before you can play a Beethoven Sonata, you must train your fingers to move across the keys in a prescribed and controlled way, often through learning scales. The movements have to become second nature, so you can eventually play scales without even thinking. When you then move to actual musical pieces, the finger skills required have been learned and can be applied to the making of real music.

It's really about developing an unconscious memory through repetition. The goal is to reach a point where you no longer have to think about the specific details of what you are doing. It becomes second nature, and now whenever you are presented with the opportunity to perform, you can truly make music.

The Definition of Practice

There are multiple definitions of the word practice in the dictionary, but for our purposes we will look at two of these.

Definition 1: repeated performance or systematic exercise for the purpose of acquiring skill or proficiency: *Practice makes perfect.*

Definition 2: the action or process of performing or doing something: *to put a scheme into practice.*

Miraculous Ideas

In our piano example, the first definition is the time we spend at the keyboard playing scales and musical pieces over and over in order to improve our abilities. We practice piano to get good at it. The second definition relates to our need to find time and venues where we can perform piano music and reap the joys of making real music, once we have acquired the necessary skills.

In a similar way, one can practice forgiveness. There are specific techniques you can learn, and through repetition, you can improve these techniques, so that the process of forgiving can become second nature. Of course, along with the technique, there needs to be a willingness, and we'll discuss this as well.

The two meanings of practice also come into play in our practice of forgiveness. We need to learn how to forgive, through the teachings of the Course, and we need to put forgiveness into practice, overcoming the ego's attempts to prevent us from forgiving. There will be resistance, so we will have to keep the ultimate goal we are seeking in mind as we learn how to forgive.

The Technique of Forgiveness

> Ask not to be forgiven, for this has already been accomplished. Ask, rather, to learn how to forgive, and to restore what always was to your unforgiving mind. (T-14.IV.3)

Before we can practice forgiveness, we must first learn how to forgive, a technique we can repeat over and over to hone our skills of forgiveness. In reading the Course, the process of forgiveness is presented in various ways, but for our purposes we'll focus on a specific technique that can be used repeatedly in many different situations. As long as you follow the basic plan and understand the goal, you can feel free to make minor adjustments to suit your particular way.

The technique will involve three basic steps. The first is to learn to connect with the Holy Spirit within your mind. Next we will identify a specific non-loving thought where we know forgive-

The Practice of Forgiveness

ness is required. Finally we will apply a simple procedure to forgive, using the help of the Holy Spirit to overcome any resistance.

Step 1 - Connecting with the Holy Spirit

The first step in our technique is learning how to connect with the Holy Spirit. The Holy Spirit is simply the part of our self that remembers our connection to God, the part of us that knows only truth and knows only love.

The Holy Spirit is present within all of our minds and can be perceived in different ways. Some may see a loving God-like figure, others may see an inner guide, but no matter how you see the Holy Spirit, you must look within the mind. There is nothing real outside the mind, so the Holy Spirit, our connection to the Mind of God, must be found there.

The first task on the path to forgiveness is to experience this Holy Spirit, a little glimpse of the wonder of God. Take a moment and think on the place in your mind where you know there is peace and love available to you. You may initially only be able to feel this place for a fleeting moment, before the ego fills your mind with all of its non-loving thoughts.

This is the first thing you will need to practice on a regular basis, taking some time every day to just sit quietly and call on the Holy Spirit. It's a kind of meditation where you look within, asking for the place of love to show itself. By practicing this regularly you will begin more and more to know and feel comfortable in this place.

Step 2 - Identifying a Non-Loving Thought

Once you've made the connection to the Holy Spirit, no matter how small it may seem, you can begin the process of forgiveness. The next step is to identify within your mind a non-loving thought. This can be a thought of anger, fear, guilt, pain, or any other thought where you feel upset or discomfort with someone or yourself or some experience.

In selecting this non-loving thought, it is important to not be selective in the choice. Often the first thought that comes to mind will be the one to work on. You want to be careful not to reject a thought because you think it is too trivial, or on the other hand reject one that you worry might be too painful to look at. Your ultimate goal is to try to forgive everything, so starting with what is in your mind at this moment is usually the best approach.

Let's try an example. Think about a non-loving thought you've had in the last day or two – any thought with feelings of fear, anger, guilt, etc. associated with it. Bring that thought to the front of your mind, focusing on it intently. Feel all the emotions surrounding it. If possible, imagine those emotions as something physical, like a dark, roiling ball of ugliness.

Step 3 - Forgiving the Experience

Now holding that focus, begin to forgive everything associated with this experience. We have learned from the Course that all these feelings and thoughts are illusions presented to us by the ego. Knowing that, forgive each person with any connection to these thoughts, saying "I forgive..." followed by the person's name, repeating it several times. Then forgive the experience itself, saying "I forgive..." followed by what you call the event, and then "... knowing this is just an illusion created by the ego."

Next take that roiling ball of ugliness, with all the emotions tied into this experience and hand it off to the Holy Spirit, who remembers your place in the Mind of God and knows these emotions and thoughts are illusions with no power whatsoever. This will release the experience, the emotions, and the non-loving false thoughts. The ego loses some of its hold on you as your awareness of the Holy Spirit reminds you of where you belong.

The Practice of Forgiveness

As one final step, say "I forgive myself", for it was you, as your ego self, that had all these thoughts and emotions originally. By forgiving yourself, you release yourself from the heavy weight of responsibility and guilt for this negative experience, and because of this you will naturally feel closer to the Holy Spirit.

Practicing Forgiveness

Once you have completed this, select another non-loving thought and follow the same procedure. In this case you might try something further in the past, perhaps something in a relationship that has bothered you for years. The process is the same no matter when the thought and associated emotions first occurred. It is still an illusion and the Holy Spirit stands ready to release you from it.

As you choose these thoughts, remember every non-loving thought can be forgiven, no matter how strong the emotions are attached to the thought. Try to choose these thoughts as randomly as you can. This will help keep the ego out of the process of choosing. The ego will want you to only forgive certain things so it can maintain a core of non-loving thoughts. By not being critical in what you choose, you can better bypass the influence of the ego.

Now you're ready to begin a regular practice. Set aside a brief time every day to forgive a few of your non-loving thoughts. After a while, you can increase this process to several times a day as it becomes more and more natural. Eventually you may find yourself doing it without having to think about it too seriously.

Putting It All Into Practice - Continual Forgiveness

Once this daily practice becomes second nature, you can begin to apply the technique in real-time to events in your life. The ultimate goal is for you to realize when non-loving thoughts occur and to instantly forgive them. This can lead to a state of contin-

Miraculous Ideas

ual forgiveness, a state where every unpleasant experience in your life is immediately turned around through forgiveness.

Think about it. All the fear, pain, anger, sadness, guilt that you've felt over the years being instantly forgiven. This state of continual forgiveness will lead to the state of peace the Course talks about, for if all your non-loving thoughts are being forgiven, the ego has lost its hold on you, and all that will be left is love.

You will experience resistance along the way, since the ego will not let go easily. So it's important that you maintain your intent and focus to overcome the obstacles placed in your way. You must put forgiveness into practice, applying it to all the events of your life, if you want to free yourself from the ego's hold.

> You are not asked for total dedication all the time as yet. But you are asked to practice now in order to attain the sense of peace such unified commitment will bestow, if only intermittently. It is experiencing this that makes it sure that you will give your total willingness to following the way the course sets forth. (W-Intro.181-200.1)

So maybe practice, practice, practice isn't such a bad thing after all. If practice, through both learning the technique and performing the act, frees us from the ego and brings us closer to the Love of God, why wouldn't we do it? So get to work practicing forgiveness. You have everything to gain.

Looking for Love

At its core, *A Course in Miracles* is about love. It's about a state of peace where all you feel is love toward everything and everyone, and all you see in the eyes around you are feelings of love. One of the things that draws so many people to the Course is this message of love and that this love is our essence and our right and our destiny.

We are promised throughout the Course that God is Pure Love and our True Self is at home within the Mind of God. We are ultimately God's Creations and our natural experience is a love that is unimaginable to us in our current separated, ego-influenced world, a love beyond anything we experience in this world.

But even though we are promised this loving experience, the curriculum of the Course, the part of the Course which teaches us how to achieve this state of love, is not about trying to find more love in our lives. It doesn't teach us how to love someone more or how to find only loving experiences. What it teaches us is how to find the obstacles the ego has built in our mind to prevent us from experiencing the love that is our Natural State.

> Your task is not to seek for love, but merely to seek and find all of the barriers within yourself that you have built against it. It is not necessary to seek for what is true, but it *is* necessary to seek for what is false. (T-16.IV.6)

It's very clear – looking for love is not the answer. The answer is in looking for the barriers. So what are these barriers the ego is putting in our way? They're all the thoughts we have which are not loving thoughts. This includes every thought of attack, fear, pain, anger, sadness, guilt, discomfort, anxiety, unease – you name it. This includes thoughts about others and thoughts about yourself. These are all the thoughts the ego feeds us to keep up the illusion of separation.

We all recognize these thoughts. We all know how to find them. They will raise their ugly heads every day of our lives. Right now you can stop and think about what has happened to you in the last day or so, and find many of these thoughts. When you consider a lifetime, there are more than enough for us to work with. This is the first step on the road to what is true – we have to seek for what is false.

One way to begin this process is to make a list of these non-loving thoughts you have throughout the day, whether these are about current things going in your life, or feelings about long-past events. By building this list, you will take the time to focus on them. The ego doesn't want you to pay attention to what it is doing in your mind, so this is one way to foil the ego's plan. Let's look at some examples of non-loving thoughts.

Anger

We'll start with the anger we feel toward strangers. In modern life we are inundated with news reports from a variety of sources telling us about all the terrible things people do. We hear of murderers and rapists and child molesters. We hear of government leaders who treat their people badly, who steal and cheat. We hear of powerful rich people exploiting others. In all these cases our first reaction is often one of anger.

Then there are those we interact with in our everyday lives. There's the boss who makes unreasonable demands on us. There's the mother who is always criticizing us. There's the wife or husband we love, but who drives us mad at times with some behavior. There's the child who seems ungrateful for all the sacrifices we have made. Again we react to these events with anger.

The Course says the following – All anger is nothing more than an attempt to make someone feel guilty... (T-15.VII.10). Our re-

Looking for Love

action of anger is our attempt to make these individuals feel guilty, clearly not a loving thought. This anger is one of the barriers to love, and it is this anger we must forgive if we are to find real love in our lives.

Fear

As we observe animals in nature, we see predators and prey. We see animals running in fear to avoid being killed. It appears as if we have evolved from pre-historic humans who were often the prey as well, and we seem to have inherited this fear response. For most of us, though, a confrontation with a predator in the wild will never happen. Our modern civilization has insulated us.

Today we have new fears. We fear other humans who may want to attack us in order to steal our property or out of what looks to be shear madness. We fear some of the machinery of modern life, like cars and airplanes, that we know can crash and maim or kill us. We fear the emotional or psychological attacks we experience from those around us.

There are also more subtle internal fears. We may feel a lack of self worth, and fear we may fail in some endeavor. We may fear we cannot find love in life or worry about our financial position. In all these cases, the ego is showing us an illusion of who we are in order to further the idea of separation.

One of the most basic fears is the fear of death. The ego has projected the illusion of bodies inhabiting a physical world. The one certainty in this illusion is that all of these bodies will die, including our own. When we are younger we worry about death through accidents or illness, but as we age, we know we are moving ever closer to the time our bodies must die. There is an inevitability to death that permeates our existence here.

The Course tells us that though these fears appear real, they are only meaningless projections from the ego, and every one of these fears is a barrier to our experience of love. There is in reality nothing to fear – not attack, not failure, not death. We are Creations of God, and therefore are as eternal as God is eternal.

Guilt

We see guilt all around us, because we project guilt onto the world. When we see someone attacked, whether that attack is physical or verbal or emotional, we think the attacker must be guilty. When we are attacked, we believe that attacker is guilty. It is the ego that is telling us this, and we are willing listeners.

No matter how hard we try to be a 'good' person, we will on occasion do things we believe are hurtful to others. When we do, we inevitably feel guilty. This is the ego telling us we are not always a 'good' person, and we should feel guilty about what we have done. By getting us to focus on the guilt we feel, the ego increases our feeling of separation from others. We don't want others to see what we have done, so we hide this part of ourselves.

All of this guilt comes ultimately from the guilt we felt when we started believing in the separation. We felt guilt at having rejected the Loving God from which we came, and that deep-seated guilt is the basis for the guilt we feel inside or perceive in the external world. All of this guilt is another barrier keeping us from experiencing love.

Forgiving the Barriers

The curriculum of the Course does provide a cure for these non-loving thoughts, the idea of forgiveness. Through forgiveness, we can begin to break through the ego's barriers, to see those false thoughts as the illusions they are. Forgiveness is our path away from the ego and toward love, our path through the barriers to the love beyond.

We begin this process by learning to recognize the non-loving thoughts in our mind, the anger, the fear, the guilt. Each instance provides us with an opportunity for forgiveness. Make

Looking for Love

your list of these non-loving thoughts. When we apply the practice of forgiveness, we can take these thoughts, these barriers, and with the help of the Holy Spirit, realize the illusion of what we thought we had experienced. Once we do, we bring ourselves ever closer to finding love in our lives, the true, unconditional love toward everyone the Course tells us is our destiny.

So ultimately, looking for love is about looking for all the places in your life where love isn't. It's about finding all the non-loving thoughts and emotions, and forgiving the experiences associated with those feelings. Once that forgiveness takes place, you will be on the path to returning to your Natural State of Being, a state of Pure Love.

Finding the Holy Spirit

One of the implications of the idea of separation is the illusion of a split mind. We believe, imagine, dream that there is a part of our mind that is separate from God. This part is the ego, and as we live in this imagined world, we listen to the ego as we make our day-to-day decisions. We believe the ego has our best interest at heart, and we believe that without the ego, we would not be able to survive in this world.

If the ego is the part of the split mind that focuses on the separation, there must be another part that can't see the separation, that sees only our Oneness within the Mind of God. That part is called the Holy Spirit in the Course. It is essential if we want to see beyond the ego's world that we find this part of our mind, this Holy Spirit. For it is with its help that we can begin the practice of forgiveness and find our way Home.

An essential step in the practice of forgiveness is getting in touch with the Holy Spirit. If we only listen to the ego, we cannot achieve complete forgiveness. Without complete forgiveness, we will continue to choose the ego's view of the world, the world of attack and guilt and fear we believe we live in. With complete forgiveness, we can be free of this world and re-experience our True Self within the Mind of God.

So how do we find this Holy Spirit within? Where has it been hiding all these years? Why doesn't it just speak up so we can hear it? Is it just so ethereal we can never grasp hold of it?

What Is the Holy Spirit?

In simplest terms, the Holy Spirit is the connection between the separated world we believe in and the Home within the Mind of

Finding the Holy Spirit

God our True Self has never left. Since we believe so thoroughly in all the illusions the ego has presented to us, we need help in finding our way to forgiveness. The Holy Spirit offers that help. The Course refers to the Holy Spirit as the Communication Link between the illusory world of the ego and the real world of God.

> Being the Communication Link between God and [the separated self], the Holy Spirit interprets everything you have made in the light of what He is. The ego separates through the body. The Holy Spirit reaches through it to others. (T-8.VII.2)

> The Holy Spirit is your Guide in choosing. He is in the part of your mind that always speaks for the right choice, because He speaks for God. He is your remaining communication with God, which you can interrupt but cannot destroy. (T-5.II.8)

This place within the mind is always available to us. We spend our days listening to the ego telling us what to do in life. We look to the outside world for fulfillment and to outside relationships for emotional happiness. The ego tells us that is where our fulfillment lies. But the ego is telling us a tall tale, a great myth that we have been too willing to believe in.

This Holy Spirit within is where the only true fulfillment and happiness can be found, for it always has our best interest in mind. It knows we can only achieve peace and joy by remembering our connection to God. We have a choice to make.

> The Holy Spirit, like the ego, is a decision. Together they constitute all the alternatives the mind can accept and obey. The Holy Spirit and the ego are the only choices open to you. God created one, and so you cannot eradicate it. You made the other, and so you can. Only what God creates is irreversible and unchangeable. (T-5.V.6)

Miraculous Ideas

Your Willingness

The Holy Spirit asks only your small willingness, a simple intent to find another way. We are all weary in this world because we have listened to the ego for too long. Out of this weariness, we must search for new direction, the direction back to our Home in God. The Holy Spirit is your path to that Home.

> The Holy Spirit cannot ask more than you are willing to do. The strength to do comes from your undivided decision. There is no strain in doing God's Will as soon as you recognize that it is also your own. (T-2.VI.6)

> Offer the Holy Spirit only your willingness to remember, for He retains the knowledge of God and of yourself for you, waiting for your acceptance. (T-10.II.2)

This willingness will bring you the peace you desire. Finding the Holy Spirit is not about searching, but about intending. When you make that clear intention, you must find what has always been waiting within your mind. God intended you to find this path back Home, and He has only waited for our intention to match his.

> God can communicate only to the Holy Spirit in your mind, because only He shares the knowledge of what you are with God... Everything else that you have placed within your mind cannot exist, for what is not in communication with the Mind of God has never been. Communication with God is life. Nothing without it is at all.
> (T-14.IV.10)

As we learn to forgive and put that forgiveness into practice, we will on a daily basis be strengthening our connection to the Holy Spirit. We will more and more begin to follow the Will of the Holy Spirit, which is ultimately the Will of God. We will make decisions with the help of the Holy Spirit and no longer feel we

Finding the Holy Spirit

are completely on our own. We will begin to weaken the ego's hold on us.

> There is another advantage, and a very important one, in referring decisions to the Holy Spirit with increasing frequency. Perhaps you have not thought of this aspect, but its centrality is obvious. To follow the Holy Spirit's guidance is to let yourself be absolved of guilt. (M-29.3)

When we are no longer alone in our decisions, no longer alone in how we relate to those around us, and at peace with our place in the world, the guilt we have felt in this life will melt away. Without guilt, the ego has no power. Without guilt, we are at last on our way Home.

A Simple Meditative Technique

One way to get more in touch with the Holy Spirit is through a peaceful meditation. There are many different ways to envision the Holy Spirit within, but we will explore a simple visual meditation as one means for contact. Though it may seem like you are just using your imagination in this exercise, it is important to remember the Holy Spirit is very real, more real than anything in your life.

Begin by sitting in a quiet place free of distractions. Get comfortable, close your eyes and take a few deep breaths. At this stage the only thing you need to do is to relax as much as possible. The relaxation allows your mind to begin to free itself from the ego's influence. Start with your feet and toes and work your way up the body relaxing each part until you reach the top of your head. Continue to breathe easily.

Now imagine that your mind is a large space above and including your head. Within this space thoughts are flying around in all directions. The space is huge, extending in all directions and without boundaries. Take a few moments to just feel this space, this mind that is your current experience. Observe all the

Miraculous Ideas

thoughts without fixating on anything. Just be aware of the motion.

Next imagine all the thoughts from the left side of your mind begin to migrate over to the right side. Slowly but steadily these busy thoughts, like bees buzzing around, move over to the right side of your mind. As this occurs, the right side becomes a hive of activity, thoughts of everything physical and emotional flying around. This wild motion is what your everyday thinking is like.

Over on the left side, as the thoughts migrate away, there is a peaceful emptiness remaining. There may be a few stray thoughts around, but the peace is clearly there. Imagine a soft, comforting light filling that empty space. Now imagine that the center of who you are moves over into that peace, taking up residence within that light and peace.

That peace is the Holy Spirit, your connection to God. Experiencing this place puts you in touch with the memory of your True Home. Once you find this place, you will have a new home you can go to whenever you need to get away from the crazy ego world of pain and guilt and fear. Simply feel this place for as long as you like.

Practice this meditation regularly and then when you practice forgiveness, you will be more able to find the Holy Spirit, whether as this peaceful place or more as a spiritual personality you can talk to. The Holy Spirit knows the non-loving thoughts you are forgiving are all illusions, and these illusions will disappear as you remember where you came from.

Using the Workbook and Manual for Teachers

The Workbook of the Course provides you with 365 daily lessons that guide you gently through the process of changing your perception. Along the way you will be encouraged to get in touch with the Holy Spirit, and to turn more of your everyday decisions over to the Holy Spirit, who always has your best interest in

Finding the Holy Spirit

mind. This, combined with practicing forgiveness in your life, will bring you greater peace, and you will be on the road Home.

> If you are not a body, what are you? You need to be aware of what the Holy Spirit uses to replace the image of a body in your mind. You need to feel something to put your faith in, as you lift it from the body. You need a real experience of something else, something more solid and more sure; more worthy of your faith, and really there. (W-91.7)

Forgiveness is key to our freedom and to finding our way Home.

> *Forgive, and you will see this differently.* These are the words the Holy Spirit speaks in all your tribulations, all your pain, all suffering regardless of its form. These are the words with which temptation ends, and guilt, abandoned, is revered no more. These are the words which end the dream of sin, and rid the mind of fear. These are the words by which salvation comes to all the world. (W-193.5)

> The mind that serves the Holy Spirit is unlimited forever, in all ways, beyond the laws of time and space, unbound by any preconceptions, and with strength and power to do whatever it is asked. (W-199.2)

And from the Manual, comes this.

> To ask the Holy Spirit to decide for you is simply to accept your true inheritance... If you have made it a habit to ask for help when and where you can, you can be confident that wisdom will be given you when you need it. Prepare for this each morning, remember God when you can throughout the day, ask the Holy Spirit's help when it is feasible to do so, and thank Him for His guidance at night. And your confidence will be well founded indeed. (M-29.5)

Miraculous Ideas

The Course never wavers on this point – the Holy Spirit resides in every separated mind, and we all have the ability to touch that Spirit, and through this contact, to radically change how we see, feel, and think about everything in this world. Finding the Holy Spirit is the most inevitable thing in your life. It is only up to you to decide to start looking.

There Is Only One Mind – And Only One Ego

It is fundamental in the Course that God is Pure Oneness and God is Mind and only Mind. Any thoughts of duality or of any kind of reality outside of God is an illusion, a wayward thought. It is through the idea of separation that we have become enmeshed in what seems to be a haphazard, sometimes insane reality. And it is the ego that keeps the separation illusion going.

The One and Only Ego

In the Course, the phrase 'the ego' appears more than 400 times. The word 'egos' appears only 7 times, mostly in Chapter 4, 'The Illusions of the Ego'. Clearly the focus of the Course is on seeing the ego as a whole, as one complete entity, and not as billions of individual egos. My ego and your ego are simply the ego, not a collection of separate egos having separate thoughts.

It all starts with the idea of separation and the group of thoughts that a part of God can actually separate from God. This leads to the separated self, the feeling of being a self separate from God, what the Course tells us is the fundamental illusion. The part of the separated self that focuses solely on maintaining that illusion is the ego, the one and only ego. This ego uses whatever means it can to keep us focused on all the pain and anger and guilt in the world so we will believe we are truly separate.

In order to further distance itself from the True Self, the separated self created the illusion of the great split, the one ego becoming billions of individuals. These individuals see themselves living in a world with other individuals. We appear to be isolated, separated personalities, but this is just another illusion created by the one ego. No matter how obvious this appears to be, all of those individuals in the world are part of a whole.

If another person gets angry with you, you may feel anger or fear or guilt as a response. You feel this person is someone separate from you, with separate thoughts and feelings. Even as you view this situation from the point of view of the Course, you see this as one ego attacking another. But there truly is only one ego, and when we perceive someone attacking us, it is simply a part of the ego attacking itself.

This fundamental point can help to free us from the influence of the ego. One of the ego's main tools is for us to see the others we share this world with as separate individual beings, with separate individual thoughts and choices. If we can somehow begin to see this as all part of the one ego, then an important ego tool has been lost, and we can potentially see how as we choose the ego, it is the one separated self choosing the ego.

The Meaning of One Ego

There are many consequences to this. For instance, if there is only one ego, then those billions of egos are part of one entity. This means that every thought that you have is known by every part of the ego, and likewise you, as part of the ego, know every thought of every other part of the ego. You may try to hide this knowledge from yourself, but those thoughts are there nonetheless.

This shared thinking means that we are essentially a collective mind. What seems to be separate thought is an illusion, and as we go through life, we are in constant communication with everyone around us. This may be beyond our everyday awareness, but we can, if we pay attention, discover some of these shared thoughts.

This is a simple explanation for intuition, for clairvoyance, for any mental phenomenon where knowledge of the thoughts and feelings of others is concerned. The fact that some people feel

There Is Only One Mind – And Only One Ego

greater intuition about others, or are more aware of events that are perceived beyond the normal five senses, is simply because some individuals have fewer mental barriers preventing them from seeing the totality of the ego.

One of the results of studying the Course is a feeling of greater empathy with those around us. We begin to see the others we share this world with as less threatening and more deserving of our love and respect. We begin to look past the separateness the ego shows us, and see these others as like ourself, merely on a journey, sharing a common goal.

Another result of the one ego relates to the idea of reality creation – that we fundamentally create our own personal experience. This idea is in complete agreement with the Course, in that the Course says that what we perceive is what we project. We first have the idea, and then we experience that reality. By realizing there is only one ego, then whenever we are expressing ego-like behavior, or we see this behavior in others, what we express and what we observe comes from the same place.

One problem with the concept of reality creation has always been – How do I create my reality with you in it, and you create your reality with me in it, and somehow it all agrees? With the idea of only one ego, then reality creation becomes the one and only ego creating one and only one reality. There is no possibility of conflicting realities, so when I create what appears to be my reality, it is simply part of the one ego creating its one reality.

Of course, ultimately what this leads to is the realization that we are not individual personalities, that when we think and act and perceive, we are simply part of the one ego mind that is thinking and acting and perceiving through all these illusory individuals. This idea can be scary at first, since we fear the loss of our individual selves with the ability to make our own personal individual decisions. The reality is that it is the one separated self that is making all of these decisions, and as long as we give power to the ego, we will feel trapped in this illusory reality.

Freeing Ourselves from the One Ego

So how do we break free of all of this? We first must realize that the ego is only part of the separated self. There is another part of the mind that has never lost the awareness that the separation idea is an illusion. This is the one and only Holy Spirit, our connection to God that can lead us on the path back to our True Self, the Self that knows only the Oneness of God.

Ultimately we do have one choice in this life, to choose to let the ego make our decisions for us, or to choose the Holy Spirit. When we choose the Holy Spirit, we can finally be led away from the ego's illusory world. That world is the source for all the pain we experience in this life, and it is our connection to the Holy Spirit that can release the pain.

It is all those non-loving thoughts the one ego presents to us, all the thoughts of fear, anger, attack, and guilt, that we can be free of through our connection to the Holy Spirit. It is through the act of forgiveness, of realizing these thoughts truly are illusions, that we begin to choose another way, the way of God and the Holy Spirit.

By following the practice of forgiveness, you can change your life away from one of conflict, fear, and guilt to one of love and peace and connection to God. These are not fairytale ideas, but real, practical ideas that will lead to real change. The one and only ego can maintain itself only if we choose to focus on the non-loving part of our lives. Choose for God and the Holy Spirit, and the Love and Peace of the True God can be yours.

Original Fear and Original Guilt

There is a concept in Christianity called original sin. The idea varies depending on what branch of the faith you belong to, but in essence it says that Adam and Eve sinned by disobeying God in the Garden of Eden, and that sin is passed down to one's offspring so everyone enters the world already in a state of sin, the original sin.

Original sin was not part of the theology until many years after Christ's death and the idea can be found in the writings of Paul and Augustine in the early centuries of the first millennium. In the Catholic church and some Protestant sects, this evolved into the idea that one must be baptized into the church to remove this sin. Since there was a concern that a young child might die before the sin was washed away, baptism (or christening) in the Catholic church is now done soon after birth.

For the Catholic church this idea means that we come into this world already in a state of sin, and through baptism we begin the process of washing this sin away. We will, of course, be tempted to other sins throughout our life, so the process of sin and confession and penitence is lifelong, and the result of all of this won't really be known until we die and meet the Judgment.

Coming into life with this original sin means the struggle to do God's will is lifelong. Even with early baptism, the church must educate us into understanding what is and isn't a sin and to the processes we can undertake, like confession and penitence, to try to wash these sins away. The goal is to reach the end of life with as few sins as possible that we haven't repented. God will then give us a better judgment after we die.

Miraculous Ideas

A Course in Miracles and the Separation

In *A Course in Miracles*, we learn there is something similar to this idea, the idea of separation. The world we experience, the ego world of attack, pain, guilt, fear, and all the rest began with this idea. It is this idea of separation that we inherit, not through our birth into this world, but through our continuing belief in the separation.

> The ego arose from the separation, and its continued existence depends on your continuing belief in the separation. (T-4.III.3)

Originally there was only the Natural State of Pure Love existing in the Mind of God. Then came 'the tiny, mad idea' of the separation. Could a part of the Mind of God separate itself from God? This is impossible, but the illusory belief that this could occur can be explored. This collection of illusory thoughts of separation we call the separated self. The part of this self that focuses all its energy on maintaining the separation we call the ego. It is important to remember, though this ego and the personalities this ego creates seem very real, it is all just a collection of illusions.

Original Fear and Original Guilt

In order for the ego to maintain the illusion, the experience of the True Loving God has to be denied. One way to do this is to see a new 'God' that would be angry that we had separated and would want to punish us in some way. This is a 'God' we must fear, and this therefore becomes what we will call the original fear. This original fear becomes the basis for our existence, since any re-experience of the True God would show us once and for all how the whole ego edifice of fear is an illusion.

> Before the separation the mind was invulnerable to fear, because fear did not exist. Both the separation and the fear are miscreations that must be undone... (T-2.III.2)

Original Fear and Original Guilt

In addition, this separated self now experiences the loneliness of this belief in separation, and on top of the fear comes the feelings of guilt for believing we left God behind. This guilt gives the separated self further reasons to hide from God and to reinforce the illusion of separation. This we will call the original guilt. We are now living with a fundamental fear and guilt that guides all of our decisions in this world, the decisions we make to embrace the ego.

The Great Split

In order for the separated self to free itself from this original fear and guilt, the great split occurred and the illusion of billions of individual selves all interacting in a projected external world was created. Since this world is a projection of the ego, it contains all the same illusory fear and guilt the ego experiences. Believing we are individuals living in this external world, we inherit the same illusory fear and guilt from the ego.

All of our interactions in this world with all the other individuals we see external to ourselves are just a continuation of the projection by the ego of fear, guilt, attack, pain, and other non-loving thoughts onto these individuals. We are the ego interacting with the ego in a non-loving environment. As long as we maintain this belief in the ego and the separation, we are destined to fall short in our desire for more love and peace in our lives.

Reflections of Fear and Guilt

Since there is only one separated self, which created the illusion of the billions of individual separated selves, anyone we fear is part of that original separated self. Any transgressions we feel guilty about are against that same separated self. What we fear and what we have transgressed against is that 'God' we imagined immediately after the separation. Therefore, all fear and all guilt are but reflections of the original fear and guilt.

It is these reflections of the original guilt and original fear that we see in ourselves and in others. The guilt and attack and pain in this world seem to come from myriad individual acts carried out by the myriad personalities we interact with. If we look closely though, it is possible to see that every one of these acts is just a slightly hidden version of the original belief in separation.

If this is true, then by healing any of the guilt and fear in your life, you will get that much closer to healing the original guilt and fear. And conversely, if we reach the point where we can look at the original fear and guilt we feel toward God and learn to heal it, we will be stepping back from the idea of separation and freeing ourselves from the hold of the ego.

Forgiveness of Others

The Course teaches us that the path back to the True God begins with forgiveness. This forgiveness is simply the recognition that what we believe happened to us never occurred and was only an illusory belief. By joining with the Holy Spirit within, the part of the separated self that remembers its Home in the Mind of God, we can begin to realize these instances of fear and guilt and pain and attack are all the result of that original illusion – the idea of separation. We begin the return to God by forgiving the small instances of fear and guilt in our everyday lives.

'The Practice of Forgiveness' provides the practical techniques that will help on this road of forgiveness. You can follow the three-step process of connecting with the Holy Spirit, observing a non-loving thought, and releasing the thought to the Holy Spirit for healing. By applying these steps on a consistent basis, you will naturally begin to lead a more peaceful life. Ultimately as the practice becomes constant, you can begin to live a life of continual forgiveness.

Original Fear and Original Guilt

Forgiving the Original Fear and Guilt

We begin the process of forgiveness by forgiving all the small non-loving thoughts and experiences in our everyday lives. These can be daily events or events from our distant past. These are all the reflected thoughts of the original thought of separation and the fear and guilt that came with it. These are the thoughts that are easy to find in our mind, the ones close at hand.

But at some point in this process of forgiveness, we will have to go deeper and look at that original fear and guilt, at the feelings and beliefs we have about God. This will bring us close to the final step of returning to God, since once we realize with the help of the Holy Spirit that the entire idea of separation and of a 'God' we must fear are truly illusions, the whole purpose for this ego-inspired world will go away.

When you feel you have learned the practice of forgiveness, when you have applied forgiveness to many of your past and present everyday non-loving thoughts, and when you have begun to turn to forgiveness before you choose attack, you will be ready to look at the original guilt and fear of God. You can call on the Holy Spirit to guide you in the process of forgiving these ideas and forgiving yourself for believing in them.

When we are ready to see we are not separate from God in any way, and never were, we will be ready to turn to God to show us the way back. At this very moment, God is awaiting our return, and when we accept that truth completely, He will welcome us back unconditionally to His Loving Home.

Section II: Thinking Differently

Getting What You Deserve

What do we deserve? We often talk about people deserving what they get in life, which can be seen either positively or negatively. We believe that someone who behaves a certain way and follows certain rules deserves to be rewarded. We believe someone who hurts others and goes against those rules deserves to be punished. In either case there is a sense that we should receive something, positive or negative, based on what we do and how we behave.

There is something in the world that we have accepted internally that seems to be telling us the thing we are doing is right or wrong. Then as we try to follow these ideas, we make decisions and take actions in the world that lead to a deserved reward or punishment. This appears to be the main way people act and relate within the material world.

This way of acting in the world, believing we are deserving of something, good or bad, leads us to focus on getting more rewards and avoiding more punishments. Because of this, we fail to see acts of love and kindness around us and we fail to act in loving and kind ways when we don't see a particular reward in doing so. This makes our behavior fundamentally selfish.

The Popular View

Let's take a couple of examples. Suppose Rhonda grows up in a difficult home situation, but due to some inner resolve, works hard in school, makes it to college, and starts her career. Most people would root for her, wanting to see her succeed. They feel she is deserving of monetary and other rewards. They want to see her get what she deserves.

Miraculous Ideas

Now let's consider Sharon, growing up in a similar situation, but from an early age, she blames her life situation for the reason she is not successful. She does poorly in school, eventually gets into drugs and commits a robbery in order to get money for drugs. She gets caught and is sent to jail. Most people would see her life as a failure. They feel she is deserving of her punishment. They want to see her get what she deserves.

But who decides what each of us deserves in this life? In our examples above, there seemed to be some set of rules that when followed makes us deserving of reward, and when not followed makes us deserving of punishment. But where do these rules come from? For most of us growing up in this world, these rules come to us through our parents, our friends, our church, our legal system, the media, and anywhere else we listen to others to learn how to behave.

As we make these rules our own, we begin to believe that if we follow the rules, we deserve certain rewards in our lives. These rules and rewards will vary from person to person, since not everyone agrees on the same set of rules. We will also believe that if we consistently violate these rules, we are worthy of some kind of punishment, whether that punishment is externally applied or is expressed as internal feelings of guilt.

In reality, what often happens is that as we try to meet these rules and expectations, the rewards are never as much as we had hoped. And conversely the punishments we receive may seem to be more harsh than we deserve. It's ultimately a game of frustration trying to get rewards from life and trying to avoid punishments.

The Course in Miracles View

In *A Course in Miracles* we discover a different way to see this whole process. In the Course, it all begins with the Oneness of the Mind of God. Somewhere, somehow within this Mind, the

Getting What You Deserve

illusory idea of separation occurs. That idea is explored and played out in all its many forms and variations, until we reach the illusory world we now believe we inhabit – individual bodies living in a world of form.

This world is just an imaginary idea within the mind, and the part of the mind that maintains this illusion we call the ego. The ego's task is to convince us the separation is real, and it uses whatever it can, including fear and guilt, and physical pleasure and pain. One of the ways it does this is to try to convince us there are rules we must follow to achieve happiness in our lives. The rules might be religious in context or more secular.

For example, in the religious context, something like the Ten Commandments gives a basic set of rules we are told to follow. If we do, there is the promise of having both a happier life in this world and the possibility of reaching Heaven in the afterlife. If we violate these rules in some way, there are punishments awaiting us as well.

In a more secular example, someone might have a basic humanist philosophy and believe that through altruistic actions, we are more fulfilled and more likely to receive kindnesses from others. If this person fails to follow through with some actions, they may feel guilty at not living up to the image of the kind of person they want to be.

In both of these instances there is the sense that by following the rules we operate under, we are deserving of a reward. If we fail to follow these rules, we deserve some kind of punishment. In any case, it is the ego who is setting the rules for this life, and it is the ego that will ultimately trap us in those rules, finding failure no matter how hard we try.

The ego is whispering in our ears that we deserve more from life, and at the same time, we are not worthy of more and should be punished in this life. This great confusion is the ego's tool for making sure we continue to see the separation and we continue

Miraculous Ideas

to feel disappointment in life as we fail to receive all the rewards we feel we are due.

Forgiving the Rules

The Course offers us a way out through the practice of forgiveness. In this particular case, we must start by looking at all these rules, examining each one with the understanding that the ego is the source for these rules. We need to forgive these rules and pass to the Holy Spirit all the emotions we feel because we try to live according to these rules, and often fail in doing so. The Holy Spirit knows these are just meaningless, irrelevant illusions the ego told us were of great importance.

Then we must forgive all the myriad outside influences that we believe created the rules we operate by. This includes our parents, the church, the media, the government, even our friends who influence us. One by one if you identify the source of a rule in your mind, you can call on the Holy Spirit to forgive that entity and thereby further release that rule from its influence over you.

In addition, you need to forgive yourself for believing you deserved these earthly rewards or for believing you deserved some punishment for your behavior. Once again call upon the Holy Spirit, the antidote to the ego, and release these feelings of expected reward and punishment. What you ultimately will be left with is a life without rules, a life of simple pure being.

What Do You Really Deserve?

Our ego selves will continue to argue that we are deserving of rewards and punishments as we go through life in this world. Without these rewards and punishments, life, according to the ego, would not be worth living. Society would completely fall apart. The certainty of the decisions we make would disappear. Complete chaos would be the result.

Getting What You Deserve

But from the point of view of the Course, you don't deserve any rewards in the illusory world we live in. And you don't deserve any punishment in this world either. You don't deserve anything in this world. What you deserve is to be free of these illusions through forgiveness and connecting with the Holy Spirit. What you deserve is complete union with the Mind of God. What you deserve is Love and Peace and a return to your Natural Loving State within the Great Oneness.

A Course in Miracles and the Borg

Ok, for all you Trekkies and former Trekkies out there, I know you've been looking for that fundamental link between *A Course in Miracles* and the voyage of the Starship Enterprise. At long last I believe I've found it in, of all places, the Borg. I know, I know, the Borg seems to be the true opposite of anything spiritual, but give me a minute to explain.

This all has to do with the concept of God. For most of us in the world, to the extent we are taught and grow to believe in a concept of God, we see God as something separate, something outside ourselves. Even if our souls are made of God stuff, when acting within this world, we're always making choices and being watched by God as we do. It's like we're corporate spin-offs from God with a separate identity and where the CEO of the spin-off is our individual self or ego. This self makes choices, always with free will, and these choices will someday be judged.

The judgment factor means there's a set of rules we're acting for or against, and if we understand those rules properly and chose correctly, we can achieve happiness and eventually live in some kind of Heaven. Alternatively if we make the wrong choices, we are destined to either live in Hell or to continue to reincarnate into this world over and over as we somehow work off our karma. In either case, making the wrong choice, going against the rules, will lead to unhappiness.

Even the reality creation, law of attraction concept requires some greater power, often just referred to as the Universe, to bring manifestations into existence. This Universe seems to be benign, but once again we're stuck with free will, and in this case, no

A Course in Miracles and the Borg

moral sense of what or why we're manifesting. There always seems to be some kind of physical limitation to these ideas as well. Suppose everyone in the world decided they wanted a Mercedes – could six billion Mercedes appear, and where would all that gasoline come from? There needs to be a meaningful purpose behind all of this.

The Course describes something very different – a God with a collective Mind. There is no soul, no spin-off, no separate identity or personality. This God is Everything, and within the Mind of this God, thinking is a shared process – actually more than shared, since there is nothing outside to share with – it's only God thinking with Itself. This idea of a collective Mind can be very disturbing, for in our everyday lives, there is always something separate, called myself, who is thinking.

Star Trek: The Next Generation

So, you might ask, what does this have to do with the Borg? The Star Trek: The Next Generation (TNG) TV show, like all the Star Treks, involves the exploration of space in which all manner of good and evil presents itself. Several of the episodes in TNG have spiritual themes, and these ideas became an integral part of the series.

There is one episode where Captain Picard passes out on the bridge of the Enterprise for twenty minutes, and during that time he experiences the complete adult life of a man on another planet. He learns to play the flute as this man, and when he awakens on the Enterprise, he knows how to play the flute. This experience and the flute-playing influence a number of later episodes.

In other episodes, there is an entity called the Traveler, who seems to be able to transcend space and time. He eventually has an effect on Wesley Crusher, who in the final episodes of the series goes off with the Traveler into realms unknown. Wesley also has several encounters with the spiritual ideas of what seem to be Native Americans.

But throughout the series perhaps the most intriguing of their adversaries were the Borg, who were unique in that their purpose wasn't to kill others to gain territory or resources. Their mission was to assimilate all the sentient beings they encountered in their travels through the universe, and once assimilated, these beings, including humans, would become part of the collective mind that was the Borg.

To the humans, who were perfect examples of strong, separated individuation, being assimilated by the collective mind of the Borg was the most frightening thing in the universe, more frightening than death itself. By becoming part of the Borg, one knew the thoughts of all the other Borg and one acted with the sole purpose of maintaining and expanding the Borg. The bodies of the individual Borg were depicted in the most disgusting manner, with tubes running in and out, and some kind of green liquid coursing through them.

There was one episode where a Borg became disconnected from the collective, and the entire hour was spent trying to retrain this one to think like an individual, giving it a name to distinguish it from others, teaching it to listen only to its own thoughts, and ultimately turning it into a duplicate of a human. There was never any questioning in the episode that this individual state was vastly superior to the state of collective consciousness.

God and the Borg

In many ways the Borg is similar to the concept of God from the Course – a collective mind and the possibility, at least, of becoming everything in the universe. But there is one critical missing aspect – love. The Borg were the antithesis of love. They were powerful, judgmental, hateful, and only out for themselves, but they wanted everyone else to become a part of them.

A Course in Miracles and the Borg

We can turn to the Course and the idea of separation to see how the Borg and the ego's idea of 'God' relate. The idea of separation begins with a belief that something separate from God can exist. In order to maintain this idea, the experience of the Loving God must be avoided at all costs. One way to do this is to create the idea of fear and, consequently, the idea of something to be feared.

In this scenario, God becomes the focus of the fear; for if we do not fear God and were to re-experience the God of Pure Love, the illusion of separation would fall apart. One way to create a fear of God is to see this new 'God' as an enemy who is out to harm us in some way, perhaps by judging us and potentially wanting to punish us for what we have done. This may sound preposterous, since God, by definition, is Pure Love, but it shows how absurd the idea of separation is and how much must be done to prop it up.

This new 'God' that the separation thoughts created, the fearsome, judgmental 'God,' is the most feared thing to the ego, to our individual personalities or selves. It's the most deep-seated fear we have, the original fear, and whenever we see aspects of a collective mind, the ego tells us we must avoid it at all costs. That 'God' is missing the same aspect the Borg is missing – love in its purest form.

So the story of the Borg becomes an allegory where the travelers on the Enterprise represent the ego, our individuated personality. The Borg represents the fearsome 'God' with it's collective mind and it's desire to assimilate us. In this story we must avoid this assimilation for ourselves and all others at all costs, even to the point of death.

By realizing that this 'God' is just another of the endless illusions presented to us by the ego, and by forgiving this 'God' and all the other ego illusions, we can begin to free ourselves from the ego's plan of separation. We need to throw out those old concepts of

Miraculous Ideas

'God' and accept the God as described in the Course, a God of Pure Love and Pure Mind. This new God becomes a thing of beauty and joy, a collective Mind into which we will ultimately return. It's time to ignore all those fearful images of collectivism that the ego presents to us and embrace the one and only collective, the True Loving God.

It Used to Be Nice to Feel Special

As a young child, I remember times when my Mom or Grandma would come up to me and give me a big hug, and say, "You're really special." It felt great being special. Later in elementary school, I received some awards for 'special achievement'. These were for doing something above and beyond what was expected. I was very proud of those awards as were my parents.

Then I learned about kids with 'special needs', about 'special education', and the Special Olympics. I realized other kids were special for different reasons. And there were special occasions, like birthdays or anniversaries, special moments when times were shared with others. A special could even mean a sale price at a supermarket.

As time went on, I began to wonder - given all these different ways of being special, what does special really mean? With some additional reflection, I decided it denotes uniqueness, individuality, and ultimately how one person or thing is different from another. That uniqueness might be considered exceptional or limited, but it's still unique. In this context, everyone may be considered special in some way.

Along Comes the Course

Then I discovered *A Course in Miracles*, and suddenly all my ideas of the word special were turned upside down. Now what had seemed to have been of great importance to me and to the others I interacted with – our uniqueness, our individuality, our differences – was being shown to be the fundamental problem in our perception of the world.

Miraculous Ideas

If you believe you are special, you will see yourself as being different from others in some way. If you believe someone in your life is special, you will want to treat that person differently than you treat others. This is the ego's way of showing you how you are separate from those around you, and how certain special people in your life are separate from other people.

Uniqueness means separation, individuality means separation, being special means separation. And in the Course, separation is what keeps us locked into the ego's view of the world. We see differences in others instead of realizing we are all the same, all fundamentally One Self, One Creation of God. It's the differences we must learn to forgive, and through that forgiveness, we can begin to see something other than specialness in the world.

Special Relationships

In the Course there are several long discussions about the concept of special relationships. These are divided into special hate and special love relationships. Most people understand the idea of special hate relationships, since almost everyone has experienced extreme dislike of someone or anger toward someone, and these relationships all fall in the special hate category. It seems obvious that such relationships need some kind of healing.

Special love relationships are harder for people to understand initially. Isn't the goal of the Course to have more love in one's life? Why would loving someone be a problem? It all comes down to the idea of conditional versus unconditional love. For most of the love relationships we have in this world, the ego sets conditions. The other person in the relationship should act a certain way in order for us to maintain our 'love' toward them.

But according to the Course, this 'love' is not real love at all, but a projection of one's needs onto another. If for some reason these needs aren't met, this 'love' can be fleeting, waning and waxing with the particular circumstances of the relationship within our

It Used to Be Nice to Feel Special

world of space and time. Often what seemed to be true love relationships will turn into hate relationships as the parties realize the conditions they set were not being met.

Special love relationships can be the most difficult to understand and change. For much of the time we spend with the special ones in our lives, we seem happy and fulfilled. We may notice small problems and annoyances, but can chalk those up to the normal ups and downs of any relationship. It is only when these small problems develop into bigger ones that we begin to realize how conditional the love has been in the relationship.

> The search for the special relationship is the sign that you equate yourself with the ego and not with God. For the special relationship has value only to the ego. To the ego, unless a relationship has special value it has no meaning, for it perceives all love as special. Yet this cannot be natural, for it is unlike the relationship of God and His Son, and all relationships that are unlike this one *must* be unnatural. (T-16.VI.1)

The Course encourages us to look at all our relationships and to understand how those small annoyances are indications of the specialness we have applied to them. We need to see how by treating certain others as being special, we are seeing them as separate from the rest of the people in our lives. The real love the Course talks about is universal and applied to everyone.

Forgiveness and Being Special

As with everything in the Course, the way to stop seeing specialness in the world or to stop maintaining special relationships, is to forgive. We need to identify those instances in our lives where we are seeing others as special, as different, and ultimately as separate. We need to realize that this difference is a fundamental illusion that prevents us from seeing the Wholeness that is truly there.

Miraculous Ideas

We need to apply the practice of forgiveness to these special relationships. First identify those relationships in your life where being special or separate is important. Then one-by-one forgive everyone involved, including yourself, calling on the Holy Spirit to release the specialness so the real love can be seen. If you do this regularly and consistently, the relationships in your life can change in dramatic ways.

The Course tells us,

> The Holy Spirit knows no one is special. (T-15.V.5)

It doesn't get any clearer than that, 'no one is special.' Now all the efforts we make throughout life to be unique and special and wonderful are only manifestations of the ego. All of the differences we see in others, the things that make them special, are seen to be illusions. The ego has told us that being special is important, and the more special we are, the better.

The Course says the exact opposite. What matters is what is the same about everyone, and the only absolute that is the same with everyone is that we are all Children of God. We are fundamentally God's Creation, and this illusory world we think we live in is built upon the illusion that we are separate from that God. It is built on the simple idea that we are somehow special and different from that God.

So now the realization sets in – it's not really nice to feel special. It's not good to be different. It's definitely not loving to see separation in the world. We have a role to play here and that role is simply to forgive these separation illusions wherever we see them. When we do, we will see God in everyone and love will permeate our lives.

"He's a God-Fearin' Man"

Growing up in West Virginia in the heart of America's Bible Belt, I frequently heard statements like "He's a God-fearin' man" and "That'll put the fear of God in him". Though my upbringing was middle-class and my church was middle-of-the-road Protestant, most of the kids I went to school with and people on the local TV shows we watched used such phrases when talking about their fundamental religion.

The Fear of God

In that world, to call someone a "God-fearin' man" was actually a supreme complement. The idea was that if someone was sufficiently fearful of God's wrath, he would act in a high moral way. It was therefore the job of the church to teach this fear to the parishioners, so that they would act in the proper way. Conversely, if someone was not in such fear of God, it was assumed he would have loose morals and would be more likely to commit immoral acts and crimes and blasphemies.

This all came down to a belief that there would someday be a judgment from God on all that we've done in this life. If we don't fear that judgment, we won't follow God's directives, as delineated in the Bible, and will therefore be judged harshly when the time comes, perhaps being sent to eternal damnation. Instilling this fear was an important part of the process of raising children.

This idea of fearing God is in varying degrees a part of all of the Jewish, Christian, and Muslim sects. Though God can be seen as loving, this love seems to be conditional on our behaving in certain ways. Whether it's through ritual worship or good deeds or right actions, we must do certain things in order to receive God's love. Even more troubling, if we don't properly meet these conditions, we will disappoint God and receive God's wrath.

This wrathful God is present throughout the Western religious texts. Stories from the Old Testament of the Bible are rife with men behaving in blasphemous ways and God raining down pain and destruction on them. Even in the New Testament, there are many stories of anger and attack and of a God who would allow his Son to be crucified. This must be a God to be feared.

The Course and the Fear of God

In the Course, the ego is the part of the mind solely focused on maintaining the illusory idea of separation. The ego will use whatever it can, including fear, guilt, pain, and perceived attack, in order to lock us into this illusion. It is through our belief in separation from God and in separation from each other that we find ourselves immersed in this sometimes insane life we seem to be living.

One of the fundamental barriers the ego creates is between the self we believe we are in this illusory world and the true Oneness of God. This true God is unconditionally Loving and without judgment. The ego knows if we were to fully experience the True Loving God, the illusion of separation would fall away. The ego's mission, therefore, is to prevent us from having this experience.

One of the primary tools of the ego is fear, but in order to make us fearful of God, the ego has to create an image of a 'God' that is wrathful and judgmental, a 'God' who requires certain behaviors on our part in order to receive its conditional love. In reality we never seem to be able to meet all of this 'God's' requirements and end up fearing the inevitable judgment.

> What seems to be the fear of God is really the fear of your own reality. (T-9.I.2)

"He's a God-Fearin' Man"

So then what is a "God-fearin' man"? This is someone who has bought the ego's picture of this 'God' absolutely. It's the ego that puts the fear of God in someone, simply for the purpose of preventing us from seeing we are without sin, without guilt, and ultimately without fear. And it's the ego that's trying to put the fear of God in all of us.

The religions that tell us God is to be feared are simply tools of the ego. Though all religions contain some kernels of truth, the image of God we are presented with in Western religions always includes an element of judgment and therefore an element of fear is instilled in us. It is through the ego's picture of judgment now and judgment later that binds us to fear.

Freeing Ourselves from the Fear

We are, however, not stuck with the fear. As with everything in the Course, the way to free ourselves from this fear is through forgiveness. We first must observe and recognize all the beliefs we have of a 'God' that is anything other than Pure Love. Once we observe these beliefs, we can forgive these one by one, until there is nothing left in our mind but the True God.

> For once you understand it is impossible that you be hurt except by your own thoughts, the fear of God must disappear. You cannot then believe that fear is caused without. And God, Whom you had thought to banish, can be welcomed back within the holy mind He never left. (W-196.8)

The process begins by thoroughly examining all the beliefs you have about God. It might be helpful to write these down as they come to you. Go back to your earliest days and remember everything you've been told about God, whether from your parents, the church, your friends, the media – anywhere someone has presented a description of God.

For each of these observations, determine which ones present a picture of a 'God' that is in any way anything other than Pure

Miraculous Ideas

Love. Then begin by forgiving this image of 'God', replacing it with an image of an unconditionally Loving God. Next forgive the person or institution that presented this image to you, and lastly forgive yourself for believing in this less-than-loving 'God'.

For example, suppose you were told in church as a young person that it's against God's laws to have sex outside of marriage, and you will be punished by God if you do. This punishing God is one that will love and care for you only if you follow these rules. It doesn't matter what law it is you choose, for every law imposed on you by a punishing God is worthy of forgiveness.

Now say, "I forgive my belief in a punishing God." Then "I forgive the church that presented this image to me." Finally "I forgive myself for believing that God is anything other than Pure Love." Now call on the Holy Spirit and pass off all the feelings of fear and worry and lack of self-worth associated with this belief. In doing this, your contact with the Holy Spirit will free you of these feelings, which are all illusions created by the ego to prevent you from embracing the True God.

We can continue this process by forgiving any other non-loving thoughts we have about God. Choose another rule and again apply this process of forgiveness. In time these rules will begin to fade away, and as they do, a new picture of God will emerge – a beautiful, Loving experience of Oneness. This is a God that will never judge us or punish us because we have never done anything wrong. We are without guilt and without sin. In time, we will free ourselves from the ego's picture of God, and when we do, we'll be "God-fearin'" no more.

> When the fear of God is gone, there are no obstacles that
> still remain between you and the holy peace of God.
> (W-196.12)

On the Death of Children

Somewhere in the world, children die every day. It may be through illnesses like dysentery, cancer or a failed heart. It may be from the conflicts of men in Syria, the Congo, or on the streets of an American city. It may simply come from an everyday accident like the intersection of a car and a bicycle or a pedestrian. Somewhere a child dies every day.

Or so it seems.

As we're growing up, there comes a point when we realize that people die. Perhaps someone close to us like a grandparent passes away. Perhaps we just reach an age when we begin to think outside ourselves and realize that everyone's life ends in death. We will eventually think about our own death, and wonder at the strangeness of it all.

Some of us will choose professions, like nursing or hospice care, where contact with death is a daily occurrence, but most of us don't think about death too much. After our initial realization, we put the idea of death in the back of our mind, something that's always there, but not a part of our everyday thinking.

Only when we are in a situation where death is near do we again consider it. If someone close to us dies, or if we are briefly put in a life and death moment, or if we see stories on the news of strangers dying, we are momentarily presented with mortality. We can also become immune to the emotions of what we see or read in the news, as long as we don't relate too closely to those strangers. But sometimes those dying strangers are children.

Or so it seems.

Miraculous Ideas

In *A Course in Miracles* we are presented with a different view of all of this, a way to see all this living and dying in a new light. In the Course everything real is in the mind, and what we believe we see in the external physical world is an illusion. It's a strong illusion, one we are programmed to believe in from the very beginning. It seems real to us, and life and death seem real to us.

The ego is the part of our mind that is solely focused on maintaining the illusion of separation. It's ultimately the belief in the separation that leads to our particular illusion of an external world where bodies live and die. The ego will do whatever it can to convince us this is the real world.

Within this ego view of the world, God is no help to us. He could be punishing us for some sins we have committed, even though what kind of sins seems difficult to understand at times. What sins would a seemingly innocent child have committed? Or maybe God is not punishing us, but has some greater plan we don't understand in which innocent children are snatched away from us.

Or the ego may have convinced us God doesn't even exist. In this view of the world, a world we can't completely control, death may often seem random. A tree falls on a moving car, killing someone inside. How could we possibly plan for such an occurrence? How can we as isolated, separated individuals affect such an outcome?

This is the ego's view, but the Course tells us there is another part of our mind that remembers our connection to the True God. This part of our mind knows that our true home is not this external world the ego has presented to us. This is the Holy Spirit, where we can find answers to all these questions through forgiveness.

The God of the Course is Pure non-judgmental, non-punishing Oneness. This is who we are, not the body the ego tells us is our true self. Within this Mind of God, there is only Love. The God of

On the Death of Children

the Course would not have children die. For each of us is a Child of God, and we are promised that death is an illusion, like every other illusion that grows out of the idea of separation.

It is up to us to forgive the events that the ego presents to us, those events of bodies living and dying in an external world. With the help of the Holy Spirit, we can begin to rethink these events. We can forgive all the people associated with the event. We can forgive the ego's idea of a God who seems to have made these events happen. And ultimately we can forgive ourselves for accepting the ego's way of viewing the world.

Through forgiveness, little by little we can begin to have a different emotional experience of the death we see in the world around us. As we forgive, the sense of reality of that world will begin to fade, and once it fades completely, we will return to our Home, our Natural Loving Space within the True Mind of God.

And so it is.

Section II: The Practical

Can We Really Be Guiltless?

When we look at the world outside our eyes, we see guilt in every direction. We see those who are guilty of inflicting pain on us and those who inflict pain on others. We know some people are more guilty than others. We identify with the ones we perceive as the victims in the world, and feel triumph when the guilty are finally punished.

We also see those upon whom we have inflicted pain, and who therefore remind us of our own guilt. These are the ones we get angry with, the ones we sometimes yell at or worse, and the ones we might avoid so we can try to hide from this guilt. The reminders of guilt are everywhere in that outside world, the world we believe we live in.

The answers to guilt offered to us by religion and psychology seem terribly complicated and difficult to implement. Seeking forgiveness from others, getting to the root cause of our anger and vengeance, praying to 'God' and hoping for some answer – these all seem too much trouble in our busy lives. Even when we manage to follow these solutions, often the guilt will reappear or we will experience new feelings of guilt. There seems to be little progress we can make, so most people just learn to live with guilt as a necessary part of life.

The True Nature of Guilt

But where does all this guilt come from? Ultimately it comes from us. We learn in the Course that what we are observing in the outside world is a projection from our ego/separated self. What appears to happen to others, whether inflicted by others or by ourselves, is an illusion we project and then perceive. What appears to be happening to our bodies occupying this external world is another illusion, and the hurtful things we seem to do to others are also illusions. The reality is that it all takes place within the mind.

The guilt we think we see is the guilt we actually create through our thoughts. Guilt serves a purpose for the ego. If we believe we are guilty or that others are guilty, then a world of love and peace and perfection can never be possible. It is the ego's job to keep us looking at the guilt in this world so we will remain in fear, fear for the survival of our bodies. It is also the ego's job to keep us believing we are guilty in order to hide love from us.

> Guilt feelings are the preservers of time. They induce fears of retaliation or abandonment, and thus ensure that the future will be like the past. This is the ego's continuity. (T-5.VI.2)

When we believe we see others committing wrongful acts, when we see the world awash in guilt and punishment, when we are driven by feelings of vengeance, we are giving power to the ego. This senseless cycle of new guilt and retribution for past guilt keeps the ego in control. As long as we give the ego that control through our perception of guilt, we can never be at peace in this world.

> If the ego is the symbol of the separation, it is also the symbol of guilt. Guilt is more than merely not of God. It is the symbol of attack on God… This is the belief from which all guilt really stems. (T-5.V.2)

This all started at the beginning of the original thought of separation. In order for the separated self to distance itself from thoughts of God, it had to create the ideas of fear and guilt so we would fear what had been our Natural Place in the Loving God. We would then feel guilty for believing we separated from God. It never really happened, but through guilt and fear, the ego keeps telling us it did, and unfortunately we do keep listening.

Can We Really Be Guiltless?

Freedom from Guilt

The Course does offer us a way to shut out the ego and begin to see the love that exists when the guilt and fear disappear. This is the way of forgiveness. Through the practice of forgiveness, we can remove these layers of guilt one by one until what is left is the peace we have always sought. This peace can become our way of life as the ego fades away.

You can start by forgiving all those you believe are guilty because of attacks you've perceived coming at you. These attacks can be emotional or physical, or judgments others have made of you. In all these cases you perceive yourself as a victim. Take your anger, your hurt, your upset, and pass these to the Holy Spirit, the one who knows you were never attacked, the one who will make these emotions disappear.

Next you can forgive the guilt you project out onto the world, where both the attacker and the victim are outside you. Take your outrage, your righteous indignation, your judgments of these people, and again contact the Holy Spirit to feel the release of these emotions. This is all your projection and the Holy Spirit knows that. Through this process of forgiveness you can begin to see those around you as your brothers and sisters and not just as the guilty.

Then look deeply within yourself at your own feelings of guilt. Look at all the times you believe you have hurt or judged someone. Look at the guilt you feel for what you believe you have done. Gather up every instance of this guilt and call again on the Holy Spirit to release it. One by one these instances of guilt can be forgiven, and the separation you feel from others because of your guilt, will melt away.

Finally go as deep as you possibly can and look at the guilt you feel for believing you are a part of the separation, the guilt you feel for trying to reject God. Here comes your ultimate freedom and here the Holy Spirit can help you as well. God is simply waiting for you, never judging, only Loving. If you can forgive this guilt, you will truly be ready to return to God, and to express only love in your life.

Becoming Guiltless

But how can we become truly guiltless? This seems to be one mountain too many. In fact, in most religions and psychologies, a little bit of guilt is a good thing, keeping our unbridled nature in check. In the Course, just the opposite is true. Our unbridled Nature is one of Love and Peace. Guilt serves the purpose to the ego of keeping our unbridled Nature in check as well. Only when we remove all guilt − become guiltless − can we experience this state of Love and Peace.

If we truly follow this practice, we are on the road to becoming guiltless. The Course discusses being guiltless often, and Chapter 13 of the Text is dedicated to this idea. To be guiltless is to be completely free of the ego. If we truly have no guilt, then we have never sinned or transgressed or separated. Guilt is entirely a creation of the ego, and without guilt we will be without the ego.

> The outcome of the lesson that God's Son is guiltless is a world in which there is no fear, and everything is lit with hope and sparkles with a gentle friendliness. (T-31.I.8)

The more we practice forgiveness, the closer we come to living in a state of continual forgiveness. In this state we constantly forgive the guilt we see in the world and in ourselves. Eventually we no longer see guilt in the world, we see only love. Eventually we no longer see guilt in ourselves, and we realize we can be free of all the pain and fear we felt, because we have become free of guilt.

The Course promises that guiltlessness is not only attainable, but inevitable. We were guiltless before we started believing in the idea of separation, and we will be guiltless when we stop believing in it. Without guilt, without judgment, without fear, without

Can We Really Be Guiltless?

the ego, all that's left is our Home within the Loving Mind of God.

Nothing Is Unforgivable

There are some things in the world that are just too terrible. Things that make us cringe and feel sick. Things that fill us with anger and maybe even hatred. Sometimes we hear about them from the news and sometimes they are very personal. When it's personal, we may try to hide it from others. It's just too terrible.

We often hear people say, "That's just unforgivable." or "I can never forgive him for that." For how can we forgive the terrible things that people do to one another. Things like murder, rape, genocide, all the ills in the external world we see in front of us. And how can we forgive someone who seems to intentionally want to hurt us personally, whether that hurt is something physical or merely a verbal jab.

And then there are the things we do to others in this world. We say we want to do right by everyone, but no matter how hard we try, it seems inevitable we will hurt someone somehow. We try to hide this internal guilt as best we can, but hiding it does not make it go away. We have to live with this guilt, and our actions in the world reflect these feelings of guilt.

So even if we believe forgiveness is a good idea, it's up to us to choose who and what we are going to forgive. We can work on our own little corner of forgiveness and allow that there are certain events we don't really have to address. There will always be some things that are just too horrendous or personally painful. Maybe we can just leave forgiveness of those for another day.

What's Unforgivable

But *A Course in Miracles* tells us we have to be willing to forgive everyone and everything. Can it really mean that literally? Are

Nothing Is Unforgivable

we supposed to forgive the world leaders who have people killed? How about Hitler, Stalin and their lot? What about our recent presidents, Bush and Obama, who have both ordered killing which resulted in the deaths of innocent men, women, and children. Surely we don't have to forgive all of them.

What about all the murderers, the rapists, the child molesters? We hear about a new one in the news almost every day. There can't be anything redeeming about them that would warrant our forgiveness. We have laws designed to punish them, not to forgive and let be. What kind of world would we live in if murderers were all forgiven? Surely we don't have to forgive them.

And what about that family member who is always putting me down. If I forgive him, he'll think I'm weak and just keep telling me I'm worthless. If I forgive him, he'll never change his behavior and I'll just get angry again the next time he does it to me. And I'll want to show him my anger so he knows what he's doing is wrong. Surely this is better than forgiveness.

What the Course Says

When we present all these arguments to the Course, it simply smiles back at us and says, "Nothing is unforgivable". How can this be so? In order to understand, we have to begin to look at the world the way the Course presents it to us, not the way we've been seeing it most of our lives.

It all starts with the Mind of God, our True Home. In that real world of Oneness and Love, forgiveness is completely unnecessary. Unfortunately for us, the world we believe we live in is the result of the great separation illusion, the belief that a part of God could actually separate from God. This has led to our ego mind, which projects a world for us that reinforces that separation.

In this illusory world, we believe we are bodies inhabiting an external world, a world of fear and attack and pain. We believe we must protect our bodies from the perceived evils of the world, from all the murderers and genocidal maniacs. We believe we must protect our psyches from the verbal slings and arrows meant to hurt us. And we believe we must feel guilty when we are the perpetrators of some of this pain.

Forgiving the Unforgivable

As we said, it is all an illusion, and the realization of this fact is what forgiveness is all about. It's not about letting the murderers and child molesters get away with something. It's not about letting your family members and friends hurt you at will. It's not about letting someone discover the guilt you know you are trying to hide.

Forgiveness is all about remembering, with the help of the Holy Spirit residing within your mind, where you came from. It's about remembering your True Self and its existence in the Mind of God. And it's about remembering that this ego-projected separated world you believe is home, is truly and absolutely an illusion.

Once this form of forgiveness is practiced, it will no longer matter what it is you are forgiving. It matters not whether you start your forgiveness with Hitler or with your best friend who said something hurtful to you. You can start by forgiving yourself for something you feel guilty about. It's really all the same, because it's all an illusion, the illusion of separation which has no existence, but is only a wayward thought.

When you choose to follow the practice of forgiveness, you are on the path to a radical change of perception. All these seemingly unforgivable acts will be seen in their true light, as illusory projected images presented to you by the ego. The choice to see these images is a choice for the ego. The choice to forgive and change your perception is the choice for the Holy Spirit

Nothing Is Unforgivable

Simply look for all the non-loving thoughts in your mind. Each and every one of them is an opportunity for forgiveness. Take some time each day to make a list of non-loving thoughts you have, whether they are from years ago or minutes ago. Let the list build as quickly or slowly as feels right for you. Then take some time every day to apply the practice of forgiveness to one or more of these thoughts.

When you start down this path of forgiveness, you may want to separate your non-loving thoughts into categories and only approach certain ones you feel you can handle. But from the point of view of the Holy Spirit, the severity or how non-loving a thought is, will be irrelevant. All non-loving thoughts are there to be forgiven. Ultimately you must eliminate any separating of these thoughts and approach each one without reservation.

You can begin to see every non-loving thought in the same way. Eventually categorizing thoughts into the forgivable and the unforgivable will seem silly to you. The regular practice of forgiveness shows you that no matter which thought you are forgiving, the Holy Spirit accepts the thought and never judges whether it's scary or atrocious or horrendous. It's just another non-loving thought that has no power once it is released.

When you finally reach the point where every act of forgiveness is the same, you will realize, nothing is unforgivable.

The Ego and the Monkey Mind

The 'monkey mind' is a popular term that refers to the seemingly endless monologues going on inside our heads. It's called the monkey mind, because like the activity of a monkey jumping from one thing to another, our thoughts seem to randomly jump around no matter how much we try to concentrate and control them.

For example, you might be simply walking along a quiet path and your mind will be thinking about almost everything except your immediate surroundings. Conversations you had earlier in the day, plans you have for later in the day – anything but what is going on in your present. It is this lack of focus on the present that is central to the working of the monkey mind.

Even things you see along your walk will trigger thoughts about something else. You might pass another person who reminds you of someone else, and your mind will be off thinking about past interactions with that person. The smell of a flower or plant might trigger a memory of another time, or remind you of something you're going to do soon. In either case you are taken out of your present.

Many spiritual traditions include some kind of contemplative activity. In Western religions these are more focused around prayer, and in some of the more mystical sects, this includes deep meditation. The Eastern religions use meditation as a core element of the practice, and these practices include ways to calm the mind.

The Ego and the Monkey Mind

Buddhism and Yogic Practices

The concept of the monkey mind or mind monkey comes from the Buddhist traditions of Eastern Asia. In Buddhism, one is urged to learn to retrain the mind through contemplation, to see the world as the illusion it is, and to achieve a state of peace. The ultimate goal is to awaken to enlightenment, an awareness of Nirvana, the state of pure being.

The practice of Yoga preceded the time of the Buddha by many centuries and meditation was a fundamental part of yogic practice. Today meditation is practiced in both of these traditions though there are subtle differences in approach, and some significant differences in the understanding of where the meditation is leading.

What is common is the practice of quieting the mind. In some forms of meditation, there is a mantra which is said over and over in order to focus the mind. In others there is only concentration on breathing, and in some, there is a focus on being completely in the present moment at all times. All of these states help to turn off the monkey mind, to bring the individual more completely into the present, and ultimately to achieve a state of peace.

The Ego and the Monkey Mind

The Course doesn't discuss the monkey mind, but it does refer to the chaos that is the ego's way of thinking.

> The world you perceive is a world of separation... The world you made is therefore totally chaotic, governed by arbitrary and senseless "laws," and without meaning of any kind. For it is made out of what you do not want, projected from your mind... (T-12.III.9)

What's important to understand in the Course is that the monkey mind is purposeful. It is a tool of the ego. It's not some ran-

Miraculous Ideas

dom firing of synapses or some failure in our concentration abilities. It's the way the ego uses our chaotic thoughts to create the chaotic world we believe we see in front of us. This monkey mind is the ego at work, projecting thoughts and feelings out into the world for us to perceive.

It is the chaos of these thoughts that makes the world seem so dangerous and unpredictable. If we truly are projecting the world we see, then if we can change our thoughts away from the chaos, the world we will experience will be less chaotic. In the Course, achieving peace is the goal, and that peace is in the mind. If we can stop listening to the ego and can realize attack and pain and guilt and fear are illusions, then we will discover the peace that was always there waiting.

> Yet this world is only in the mind of its maker... Do not believe it is outside of yourself, for only by recognizing where it is will you gain control over it. For you do have control over your mind, since the mind is the mechanism of decision. (T-12.III.9)

Learning to Be Quiet

Though *A Course in Miracles* is not primarily a contemplative practice, meditative elements are included. In the technique from 'The Practice of Forgiveness', it is important to experience the Holy Spirit within, and in order to do this, we must quiet our thoughts. Once we are in touch with the Holy Spirit, the full process of forgiveness can proceed.

The Course Workbook and Manual also provide a number of simple exercises for quieting the mind.

> After you have read the idea and the related comments, the exercises should be done with your eyes closed and when you are alone in a quiet place, if possible. (W-Review.I.3)

The Ego and the Monkey Mind

Three times today, set aside about ten minutes for a quiet time in which you try to leave your weakness behind. This is accomplished very simply, as you instruct yourself that you are not a body... Your will remains your teacher, and your will has all the strength to do what it desires. (W-91.5)

...as soon as possible after waking take your quiet time, continuing a minute or two after you begin to find it difficult... The same procedures should be followed at night. Perhaps your quiet time should be fairly early in the evening, if it is not feasible for you to take it just before going to sleep... If possible, however, just before going to sleep is a desirable time to devote to God. It sets your mind into a pattern of rest, and orients you away from fear...
(M-16.4-5)

The plan is fairly simple. By setting aside some time every day, you have the chance to step away from the monkey mind and focus on what really matters. To you, this may be God or the Holy Spirit or an image of Jesus. It doesn't matter how you do it, only that you do it consistently. You are showing the Holy Spirit your intent, and in changing your mind, intent is everything.

In the essay, 'Finding the Holy Spirit', there is a simple meditative technique you might use to focus away from your chaotic thoughts to the peaceful thought of the Holy Spirit. As you do, you are fundamentally changing the way you will interact with the world. Quieting the monkey mind frustrates the ego, since it is dependent on these chaotic thoughts for its existence.

As you practice forgiveness, and take some quiet time each day, you will be on the path to a different life. In time, the peacefulness that is naturally yours will take over your mind, and will be reflected in the world around you.

There is a way of living in the world that is not here, although it seems to be. You do not change appearance,

Miraculous Ideas

though you smile more frequently. Your forehead is serene; your eyes are quiet. And the ones who walk the world as you do recognize their own. Yet those who have not yet perceived the way will recognize you also, and believe that you are like them, as you were before. (W-155.1)

At Peace in the Chaos

It is important to note that the goal is to be able to forgive and touch the Holy Spirit in all kinds of situations. It is clearly easier to do this when everything around you is quiet, but if that is the only time you are able to forgive, peace will never fully arrive for you. So we use the quiet time to learn the techniques, with the ultimate goal of being able to apply forgiveness in the most chaotic situations possible. Then we will be on the road to continual forgiveness.

> This [quiet time] is emphasized for practice periods at your stage of learning. It will be necessary, however, that you learn to require no special settings in which to apply what you have learned. You will need your learning most in situations that appear to be upsetting, rather than in those that already seem to be calm and quiet. The purpose of your learning is to enable you to bring the quiet with you, and to heal distress and turmoil... (W-Review.I.4)

We can begin to heal the distress and turmoil in our lives by realizing the ego and the monkey mind are one and the same. By quieting one, you are weakening the other. Make it your goal to live in the peace inside your mind. Make it your goal to turn off the monkey mind once and for all, and hear only the soft clear loving voice of the Holy Spirit.

> Today we let no ego thoughts direct our words or actions. When such thoughts occur, we quietly step back and look at them, and then we let them go. We do not want what they would bring with them. And so we do not choose to

The Ego and the Monkey Mind

keep them. They are silent now. And in the stillness,... God speaks to us and tells us of our will, as we have chosen to remember Him. (W-254.2)

But I Don't Want to Forgive!

You go about your life feeling all fine and spiritual. You do your yoga and meditate every day. You read the Course and are going through the 365 lessons in the Workbook. You're beginning to see the world differently, realizing how the ego is directing so many of your decisions. You're working on forgiveness, knowing this practice is key to achieving peace and love in your life. You finally feel you're on the right path.

But someone, somewhere in your past, whether a few days ago or a few decades ago, treated you very badly. It may have been a physical attack, an emotional attack, or someone may have done something manipulative to hurt you. If it was a long time ago, you might not think about it very often, but when you do, the emotion of that hurt is there for you to fully experience. You've decided that this is something you should try to forgive.

As you begin to apply the practice of forgiveness, you try to immerse yourself in all the emotions surrounding that event. You may feel overwhelmed with feelings of anger and pain and sadness, and with that rush of feelings comes the thought, 'But I don't want to forgive what happened and I certainly don't want to forgive that person who did this to me.' There's almost a sense of triumph in holding back this one forgiveness from such a painful experience.

Overcoming Resistance

In the Course, we are reminded often that there is no order of difficulty in miracles, and since forgiveness is a miracle, there is no order of difficulty in forgiveness. If we can forgive one thing, we will be able to forgive anything. However in the beginning of your practice, you will often find some things easy to forgive and

But I Don't Want to Forgive!

others almost impossible to forgive. This is natural, but it must ultimately be overcome.

> No one can doubt the ego's skill in building up false cases. Nor can anyone doubt your willingness to listen until you choose not to accept anything except truth. When you lay the ego aside, it will be gone. The Holy Spirit's Voice is as loud as your willingness to listen. (T-8.VIII.8)

You need to be able to hear only one voice in your mind, the voice of the Holy Spirit. This appears to be really difficult at first. Because we have listened to the ego for so long, the ego seems almost like a friend to us – a friend who is leading us down the wrong path. Everything in the Course is there to get you to see how you have been led astray and how the Holy Spirit can lead you back. We must overcome our resistance, and when we do, the joy and peace of our True Home await us.

> To learn this course requires willingness to question every value that you hold. Not one can be kept hidden and obscure but it will jeopardize your learning... For a decision is the outcome of belief... Your decisions come from your beliefs as certainly as all creation rose in [God's] Mind... (T-24.Intro.2)

The answer for us is to find a small willingness within and to show this to the Holy Spirit. This simple willingness shows our intent to leave the ego behind and to seek a new path with the Holy Spirit as our guide. No matter how small this intent, we will find the help we need. We do not have to do it alone.

To overcome your resistance, you must first make the connection to the Holy Spirit. In a previous essay, 'Finding the Holy Spirit', we talk about ways to do this. This connection is essential, since we must have this help to overcome the ego's plan for us. The ego wants us to feel some things are too painful or too awful to forgive, and if we listen, we will always fall short on our path to finding peace in our lives.

Miraculous Ideas

The Holy Spirit is in you in a very literal sense. His is the Voice that calls you back to where you were before and will be again. It is possible even in this world to hear only that Voice and no other. It takes effort and... willingness to learn. (T-5.II.3)

So begin to put your opposition aside. See the ego's plan as a failed plan, one you are now willing to leave behind. See the Holy Spirit within as your guide and as your helper. See this new path where you turn over to the Holy Spirit your willingness to heal and to be healed, your willingness to forgive completely, no longer withholding forgiveness from anyone or any experience.

Create a List of Non-Loving Thoughts

One practical step to help you overcome this problem of seeing some acts of forgiveness being much more difficult than others, is to create a list of your non-loving thoughts. The purpose of this list is to allow you to treat every one of these thoughts equally, not putting them in any hierarchy of difficulty, but seeing each as just another opportunity for forgiveness.

You can start this simply by taking a few minutes each day and writing down on a piece of paper, or typing into your computer or other device, a list of a few non-loving thoughts you have had in the last several days. These can be any thoughts of anger, fear, guilt, pain, attack, depression, etc. You should have no problem coming up with a few of these. Write a brief description of each thought on one line and then go to the next.

The next time you do this, try going back in time a bit. This can be a few months or years or a decade or two. Take a few thoughts from these other times and write them down. Then as you continue to create this list over time, you can intermingle current thoughts with thoughts from the past. In any case, don't think about how awful one thought is versus another. It's just a list of thoughts with no ordering or filtering.

But I Don't Want to Forgive!

Once your list has reached a reasonable size, you can now apply the practice of forgiveness to these thoughts. The idea is to pick the next one at random, knowing that every one of these non-loving thoughts is equally an illusion and equally worthy of forgiveness. As you forgive each one, put a check mark or other indicator to show that you have taken care of forgiving that one. Do not remove it from the list. Just overlook these checked items when you choose your next non-loving thought.

After some time has passed and you have forgiven many thoughts, it's good once in a while to review your list. Look at all the checked thoughts and note how you feel about those thoughts compared to how you felt about them the first time you wrote them down. If you are truly forgiving with the help of the Holy Spirit, these checked items should no longer have emotional attachment for you.

Over time, as you continue this process, you may find yourself forgiving these thoughts as you write them down. You are then on the road to the state of continual forgiveness, where each non-loving thought is instantly forgiven, and the ego's power begins to fade away. You will realize your true power which is the power of forgiveness and love, and you will discover a new and wonderful peace in your life.

But I Do Want to Forgive!

When you stop to consider what you want in your life, you are really given a simple choice between two options – you can continue to live the life the ego presents you, with all the non-loving thoughts that bring you so much angst, or you can learn to forgive completely, leaving no thought and no one behind. If you make the choice for love and forgiveness, you are promising that you will forgive everyone equally, and with this promise you will have the help you need.

Miraculous Ideas

Offer the Holy Spirit only your willingness to remember, for He retains the knowledge of God and of yourself for you, waiting for your acceptance. (T-10.II.2)

To receive this help, you must only show your willingness to the Holy Spirit within. You must look beyond all the barriers you have built within your mind, all those barriers the ego tells you are so important. You must take the time to practice forgiveness and to see your brother as yourself. When you make this effort and show your intent, the outcome is assured. We will find our way Home, our Home where God is waiting for us.

It is not time we need for this. It is but willingness. For what would seem to need a thousand years can easily be done in just one instant by the grace of God. (W-196.4)

Loving Everyone

Love thy neighbor as thyself. (Bible, Leviticus 19:18)

A miracle is a service... It is a way of loving your neighbor as yourself. (T-1.I.18)

The original 'Love thy neighbor' quote comes from the Old Testament of the Bible, which means it is part of the foundation of all Western religions. Most Christians know the phrase from Jesus' comments in the New Testament, but both this phrase and the Golden Rule – 'Do unto others as you would have them do unto you' – predate Jesus' time by many centuries.

Different forms of these phrases also appear in many of the Eastern philosophies. The 'Love thy neighbor' phrase is more of a passive state, while the Golden Rule is intended to guide active behavior. In both cases the focus is on the neighbor, meaning essentially everyone you interact with in your life. It seems this act of loving everyone is, along with one's relationship with God, a key tenet of most religious thought.

But how does one go about loving one's neighbor as oneself? In most cases it seems as if we must force ourselves somehow to express this love. We need to repress all the anger and fear and guilt we feel toward others, and then turn love on when the occasion arises. It's a small wonder that people have to work so hard at this. We tend to view the ones who really seem able to completely express this selfless love as saints or great people, not like us ordinary people who must struggle with it.

Miraculous Ideas

The Point of View of the Course

This idea of loving your neighbor is a central theme in the Course as well, but the understanding of why it's so hard and the process for achieving that love are very different from conventional religions. In the Course, the word 'brother' is used most often instead of 'neighbor'. Brother is clearly used to mean everyone, no matter what the gender or age of the person. This relationship with our brothers in this world is key to all the teachings of the Course.

> No one who condemns a brother can see himself as guiltless and in the peace of God. (T-13.X.11)

> In the mad world outside you nothing can be shared... Within yourself you love your brother with a perfect love. Here is holy ground,... where only the truth in your brother can abide. (T-18.I.9)

So why is it so hard to express this love even when we know we should. It starts, as always, with the idea of separation and the resulting ego-dominated world we believe we live in. We have seen how all the pain and fear and guilt in this world is the result of the ego telling us we are separate from everyone else, a lone individual who must build up internal and external defenses to keep the dangers of the world at bay.

Some of the dangers we see are from our brothers, who we believe on occasion have the intent to harm us, whether this is some stranger out to attack us, or someone close to us who hurts us emotionally. It seems obvious there are people we must avoid and others we must defend ourselves against. As long as we listen to the ego, we will focus on the external dangers and never realize those perceived dangers all originate in our minds.

Here for once we have an explanation for why loving everyone is so hard. It's not because we lack some kind of will power, nor because we are fighting some kind of evil in the world or in our-

Loving Everyone

selves. It's because we are making an active choice every day to see the world the way we do. We are choosing to listen to the ego and not to the Holy Spirit as we make our decisions. The Course is very clear about this – the world you see is the world you project. If you see your brother as a danger to you, you have projected that image onto the world first and then perceived the danger.

Now the idea of trying to repress all the negative feelings we have about our brothers is shown to be completely futile. Those negative feelings are something we have made and to then turn around and try to suppress them is absurd. We will never be able to love another if we do not address all the negative feelings within and the ones we perceive in the world. One can never force love to happen. Love is there waiting once we let go of our ego-driven thoughts.

Forgiving Everyone

Fortunately for us, the Course takes it to the next step and offers us a clear path for removing these negative, non-loving thoughts from our minds. It is through the practice of forgiveness that we can let these non-loving thoughts go, seeing them for the illusions they are. Each act of forgiveness makes loving that much easier.

> Make way for love, which you did not create, but which you can extend. On earth this means forgive your brother, that the darkness may be lifted from your mind.
> (T-29.III.4)

In the Course, we have another advantage, the help of the Holy Spirit. We do not need to do this all alone. We don't have to figure out how we can express more love. By getting in touch with the Holy Spirit within, we will be guided as we forgive the illusions we believed our brother had committed against us. With this help, we will no longer have to try to repress our negative

Miraculous Ideas

feelings. Instead we can look all these non-loving thoughts squarely in the eye, and through forgiving every one of them, we can let the love that is our natural state come through.

> To forgive is to overlook. Look, then, beyond error and do not let your perception rest upon it, for you will believe what your perception holds. Accept as true only what your brother is, if you would know yourself... Remember always that your Identity is shared, and that Its sharing is Its reality. (T-9.IV.1)

It is this shared Identity, knowing your brother is like you, observing what is the same about you rather than what is different, that will ultimately lead you to the discovery of the love and peace within you. Through the practice of forgiveness, we begin to see all those we walk beside in this world as just like us and not as a threat in any way. It is possible to live in this world knowing that you and everyone else are safe and loved.

What It Would Be Like

As we proceed on our path of forgiveness, we can in time begin to experience continual forgiveness, where every non-loving thought that arises is instantly forgiven. When this occurs, we will no longer be in a battle with the ego, but will always be in touch with the Holy Spirit. The Holy Spirit expresses only love and when we keep the connection with the Holy Spirit in the center of our thoughts, we too can express only love.

And along with this comes the state of peace the Course promises us is our due. When you know that through forgiveness, nothing can disturb the love and peace in your mind, when you hold your communication with the Holy Spirit as central in your mind, and when you see your brother as one with yourself, you will lead a life of True Peace, miles and eons away from the ego-influenced life you so long endured.

Loving Everyone

We can now see it is how we think about our life, how we think about our brother, that ultimately determines our experience. It is our thought processes that lead us to choose between the ego's view of the world and the Holy Spirit's view. So now perhaps we can replace the 'Love thy neighbor' phrase with this phrase,

Respond to everything with love.

For it is how we respond to the events in our lives that determines whether we are expressing the ego's view or forgiveness. If we can realize in real-time our response to a situation, and can instantly replace any negative thoughts or feelings with love, we have defeated the ego in its drive to convince us we are unhappy. If we can instantly forgive every non-loving thought with the help of the Holy Spirit, we will replace that thought with love.

> In the real world there is no sickness, for there is no separation and no division. Only loving thoughts are recognized, and because no one is without your help, the Help of God goes with you everywhere. As you become willing to accept this Help by asking for It, you will give It because you want It... Ask, then, to learn of the reality of your brother, because this is what you will perceive in him, and you will see your beauty reflected in his. (T-11.VIII.10)

Suggested Reading

For further study of *A Course in Miracles*,

A Course in Miracles, Second Edition, Foundation for Inner Peace, acim.org

Navarro, Edwin, *It's All Mind: The Simplified Philosophy of A Course in Miracles*, Navarro Publishing, edwinnavarro.com

Navarro, Edwin, *The End of Guilt: Realizing Your Innocence through A Course in Miracles*, Navarro Publishing, edwinnavarro.com

Wapnick, Kenneth, *The Message of A Course in Miracles, Vol. 1, All Are Called*, Foundation for *A Course in Miracles*, facim.org

Contact the author at edwinnavarro.com.